The African American Male's: Child Support Survival Guide

Empowering fathers with knowledge, strategies, and strength to navigate the child support system — and reclaim control of their future.

Author:
Michael T. Logan

Michael T. Logan

2

©2025 Michael T. Logan
All rights reserved. No part of this publication may be reproduced, distributed, or transmitted in any form without the prior written permission of the author.

The African American Male's Child Support Survival Guide

Author: Michael T. Logan

Dedication

To every African American father who has struggled, fought, and persevered in the face of a system that often feels stacked against you—this guide is for you. May it give you the knowledge, confidence, and clarity you need to protect yourself, your children, and your future.

Preface

This book was written to provide straightforward, easy-to-understand guidance about child support in America. Too many African American men have found themselves unprepared when entering the legal system, often because of mistrust, lack of resources, or lack of clear information. The goal here is not to tell you whether child support is fair or unfair—but to arm you with the **knowledge you need to survive and thrive**.

Table of Contents

~ Chapter 1 ~ 8
Introduction – Why This Guide Matters 8
~ Chapter 2 ~ 10
A Brief History of Child Support in America 10
    Early Roots 10
    The Federal Government Steps In 10
    The Impact on African American Fathers 11
~ Chapter 3 ~ 12
Understanding Paternity – Establishment and the Law 12
    Ways Paternity Is Established 12
    Why It Matters 13
    What To Do If You're Unsure 13
~ Chapter 4 ~ 15
Custody vs. Child Support – Knowing the Difference 15
    What Custody Means 15
    What Child Support Means 15
    Common Misconceptions 15
    What To Do If You Want Custody or Visitation 16
~ Chapter 5 ~ 17
Enforcement of Child Support – How the System Works 17
    Common Enforcement Tools 17
    The Cycle of Consequences 18
    What To Do If You Can't Pay 18
~ Chapter 6 ~ 20

The African American Male's: Child Support Survival Guide

Arrears – What Happens When You Fall Behind 20
    How Arrears Build Up 20
    Why Arrears Are So Serious 21
    What To Do If You're Behind 21
~ Chapter 7 ~ 22
Jail, License Suspension, and Other Consequences 22
    Jail Time 22
    License Suspension 22
    Passport Denial 23
    Credit Reporting 23
    How to Avoid These Consequences 23
~ Chapter 8 ~ 24
African American Men and the Courtroom – Breaking the Fear 24
    Why Many Avoid Court 24
    The Cost of Avoiding Court 25
    How to Overcome the Fear 25
~ Chapter 9 ~ 27
The Debate Over Paternity Tests at Birth 27
    The Case for Mandatory Testing 27
    The Case Against Mandatory Testing 27
    What Fathers Should Do Now 28
~ Chapter 10 ~ 29
Practical Tips for Surviving the System 29
    Stay Organized 29
    Communicate the Right Way 29
    Financial Survival Tips 29

Checklist: If You're Served Court Papers	30
~ Chapter 11 ~	32
Conclusion – Taking Control of Your Future	32
Moving Forward	33
✎ Author's Note:	34

FORWARD

By *JAMES SAMUEL LOGAN*

With The African American Male's Survival Guide, Michael T. Logan offers a sublimely candid and readable witness to Black male struggle, perseverance, and reconciling integrity in the social-communal domain of child support. This Guide is indeed a very practical testimony of hope and love to Black fathers journeying through the considerable thickets of social, personal, and legal obstacles that undermine the vital child support necessary for their children to survive and flourish. On the wider scale of Black life and history with respect to child support, Logan's important guidebook makes a critical contribution not only to the lives of Black men, but also Black women and children whose lives too often and disproportionally intersect at the crossroads of persistent poverty, despair, community disinvestment, and nihilism while bearing the brunt of excessive punitive policing, obsessive community surveillance, correctional confinement, and death. And it is in the context of all this that Logan's wonderfully practical Guide knows us, speaks to us, embraces us, and compels us forward with the knowledge, in his own words, that "The child support system is tough, but with preparation and discipline, you can survive it and still be the father your child needs..."

Michael T. Logan

~ Chapter 1 ~
Introduction – Why This Guide Matters

Child support is one of the most emotional and misunderstood legal processes in the United States. For African American men especially, it often feels like a system designed to punish rather than support. The truth is, child support is supposed to ensure children are financially cared for; but without knowledge fathers can quickly find themselves buried in debt, losing licenses, or even facing jail time.

This guide matters because **too many men walk into court unprepared.** Imagine being called before a judge and within minutes you are handed a legal order demanding hundreds of dollars every month for the next 18 years. If you do not understand how child support works, the difference between custody and support, or how arrears grow; you could be trapped in a cycle that's almost impossible to escape.

For African American fathers, the challenge is doubled. Historically, the justice system has not been kind. From over-policing in communities to bias in the courtroom, many African American males avoid court altogether believing it's a losing battle. But here's the truth: **not showing up is worse than showing up.** When you fail to appear, judges often make default rulings, sometimes based on guessed income levels, which can leave you paying far more than you actually earn.

This book is not written to help you dodge responsibility. Children deserve care—financial, emotional, and spiritual. But it *is* written to help you survive the system. Knowledge is your shield. Preparation is your weapon. By reading this guide, you'll learn:

- The history of child support and how it affects African American fathers.
- How paternity is established—and why you should never ignore it.
- The difference between custody and support, and how courts see them.
- The harsh reality of arrears, and what happens if you fall behind.
- Why many men avoid court, and how to face it instead of fear it.
- The debate over mandatory paternity testing at birth.
- Survival strategies for staying ahead of the system and protecting your future.

☞ **Scenario:** *Marcus was ordered to pay $500 a month in child support. He lost his job but didn't go back to court to submit a modification for child support. Within a year, his arrears grew to over $6,000 with added interest and his driver's license was suspended, which made finding new work harder. Had Marcus gone to court immediately and requested a modification, he would've saved himself years' of struggle and financial loss.*

☞ **Survival Tip:** *Always respond to court papers, even if you don't agree with them. Ignoring the system only makes it worse.*

In short, this guide matters because it gives you the knowledge no one hands you in court. By the end of this book, you will not only understand the child support system—you'll know how to survive it, protect yourself, and still be the father your child needs.

Michael T. Logan

~ Chapter 2 ~
A Brief History of Child Support in America

To understand child support today, you need to know how it started. The child support system wasn't built overnight. It grew out of changes in family structures, welfare policies, and government priorities over the last 50 years.

Early Roots
Before the 1970s, child support was handled mostly through divorce courts. If a man didn't pay, there was little the state could do to force him. Many mothers, especially single mothers, had to rely on welfare to feed and house their children.

The Federal Government Steps In
In **1975**, Congress passed Title IV-D of the Social Security Act, creating the **Office of Child Support Enforcement (OCSE)**. This required every state to set up child support agencies. The purpose was simple: reduce the government's welfare costs by making fathers (often the noncustodial parent) financially responsible.

By the **1980s**, enforcement powers expanded. States could garnish wages, intercept tax refunds, and track parents through Social Security numbers. In the **1990s**, laws got even tougher, with the **Deadbeat Parents Punishment Act (DPPA)** making it a federal crime to avoid payments across state lines.

Today, technology allows child support agencies to cross-check everything—from your paycheck to your tax return. In some cases, even lottery winnings and unemployment benefits can be intercepted.

The Impact on African American Fathers
While the system was designed to protect children, it has often had the hardest impact on African American men. Why?

- Higher unemployment and underemployment rates make it harder to keep up with payments.
- Over-policing and incarceration remove fathers from the workforce.
- Fear and distrust of the courts cause some men to avoid hearings, leading to **default judgments**.

☞ **Scenario:** *Darnell, a young father in the 1980s, was laid off from his job. Instead of going back to court to submit a modification for child support, he simply stopped paying. Within months, the state began garnishing what little he earned from side work and reported him to credit agencies. By the time he found steady employment again, Darnell's arrears had doubled.*

☞ **What To Do If You Lose Income:**

1. **File a modification for child support immediately.** Child support does not automatically adjust when you lose your job.
2. **Provide proof** of your financial situation (pay stubs, unemployment benefits, medical records, if sick).
3. **Stay engaged** with the court—avoiding court only makes things worse.

☞ **Survival Tip:** *Remember, the system is designed to enforce payment, not forgiveness. Once arrears pile up, they rarely disappear. Your best defense is staying proactive from the start.*

~ Chapter 3 ~
Understanding Paternity – Establishment and the Law

Before child support can be ordered, **paternity must be established.** Paternity is simply the legal recognition that you are the child's father. Once it's established, you have both rights and responsibilities. If you don't understand how this process works, you could end up financially responsible for a child who isn't biologically yours—or lose your rights to be involved in your child's life.

Ways Paternity Is Established
1. **Voluntary Acknowledgment of Paternity (VAP):**
   At the hospital, both parents may be asked to sign paperwork declaring who the father is. If you sign, you are legally locked in, even if later a DNA test shows otherwise.

2. **Court-Ordered DNA Testing:**
   If paternity is disputed, the court can order a genetic test. A simple cheek swab is over 99% accurate. If results show you're the father, the court issues an order of paternity.

3. **Default Judgment:**
   If you are served with court papers but don't show up, the court can declare you the father without testing. This is one of the biggest traps for fathers who avoid going to court.

Why It Matters
- **Financial Responsibility:** Once paternity is established, child support can be ordered.

- **Parental Rights:** Legal fathers can request custody or visitation. Without paternity, you have no legal standing.

- **Permanent Effect:** In many states, once paternity is established, it's extremely difficult—or impossible—to undo.

☞ **Scenario:** *Chris was served court papers but ignored them because he didn't believe the child was his. The judge declared him the legal father by default. Two years later, a DNA test proved he wasn't the father, but the court refused to reverse the order. Chris still owes child support and arrears for a child that isn't biologically his.*

What To Do If You're Unsure
- **Don't sign at the hospital** unless you are 100% certain.

- **Request DNA testing immediately** if you doubt paternity.

- **Always show up in court.** Even if you're nervous, attendance protects your rights.

- **Act fast.** Some states only give a short window to challenge paternity.

☞ **Survival Tip:** *Never assume the system will protect you automatically. Once you're legally named the father, the law doesn't care what a future DNA test says. Protect yourself early.*

- **Voluntary Acknowledgment:** If you sign a birth certificate or a voluntary acknowledgment of paternity form, you are legally the father.

- **DNA Testing:** If you're not sure, the court can order genetic testing. Results with 97–99% probability establish paternity.
- **Default Judgments:** If you do not show up to court, the judge can legally declare you the father—even without a DNA test.

☞ **Survival Tip:** *If you're unsure, request a DNA test early. Once you're legally declared the father, undoing it is extremely difficult.*

~ Chapter 4 ~
Custody vs. Child Support – Knowing the Difference

One of the biggest mistakes fathers make is believing custody and child support are the same thing. They are not. Courts treat them as two **separate issues**, and understanding the difference can save you from frustration and costly mistakes.

What Custody Means
Custody refers to your **legal rights as a parent**:

- **Legal Custody:** The right to make decisions about your child's life (schooling, health care, religion).

- **Physical Custody:** Where the child lives and how much time they spend with each parent.

What Child Support Means
Child support is strictly **financial.** It is money you pay to help cover your child's basic needs—housing, food, clothing, school, and sometimes health insurance. Paying child support does not automatically give you custody or visitation rights.

Common Misconceptions
- **"If I pay, I get to see my child."** Not true. Visitation and custody must be established separately through the court.

- **"If she won't let me see my child, I can stop paying."** Wrong. Courts will still enforce payments even if the other parent denies visitation.

- **"If I have joint custody, I won't have to pay."** Not always true. If your income is higher, the court may still require you to contribute.

☞ **Scenario:** *Marcus and Tasha share 50/50 custody of their son. Marcus earns $65,000 a year, and Tasha earns $30,000. Even though Marcus has equal parenting time, the court ordered him to pay $200 per month in child support to balance the difference in household incomes.*

What To Do If You Want Custody or Visitation

1. **File separately.** Custody and visitation must be requested through a different petition than child support.

2. **Document everything.** Keep records showing your involvement (school pickups, medical visits, time spent).

3. **Be consistent.** Courts favor parents who show stability and responsibility.

☞ **Survival Tip:** *Never confuse money with time. Paying child support doesn't guarantee visits, and missing payments won't stop your responsibility. Treat custody and support as **two different battles** you must prepare for separately.*

~ Chapter 5 ~
Enforcement of Child Support – How the System Works

Once a child support order is in place, the state has powerful tools to make sure payments are collected. These enforcement methods may feel harsh, but they are designed to guarantee children receive financial support. For fathers, understanding how these tools work can mean the difference between staying afloat or losing everything.

Common Enforcement Tools

- **Wage Garnishment:** Money is taken directly out of your paycheck before you even see it. Employers are required by law to comply with garnishment orders.

- **Tax Refund Intercept:** If you're behind, the IRS and state tax agencies can seize your refunds to cover arrears.

- **License Suspension:** States can suspend your driver's license, professional licenses (i.e. Barber, Contractor, Nursing, etc.), and even hunting or fishing licenses.

- **Bank Account Seizure:** States can freeze or seize money from your bank account.

- **Passport Denial:** If you owe more than $2,500, you cannot get or renew a passport.

- **Jail Time:** Judges can sentence you to jail for "willful nonpayment," usually through contempt of court.

The Cycle of Consequences

Enforcement can create a dangerous cycle. For example, losing your driver's license might cost you your job, which makes it even harder to pay support. This is why staying ahead of enforcement is critical.

☞ *Scenario: Tyrone owed $8,000 in arrears. The state intercepted his tax refund, suspended his driver's license, and reported him to credit agencies. Without a license, he lost his delivery job, making it even harder to catch up. Tyrone's situation shows how quickly enforcement can spiral out of control.*

What To Do If You Can't Pay

1. **File for Modification:** If your income drops, request a change in your child support order right away.

2. **Negotiate a Payment Plan:** Many states allow payment plans for arrears to stop aggressive enforcement.

3. **Communicate with the Court:** Silence makes judges assume you're avoiding responsibility.

4. **Seek Legal Aid:** Even if you can't afford a lawyer, legal aid groups or fatherhood programs are able to assist.

☞ *Survival Tip: Enforcement never goes away by itself. If you can't pay, do not disappear. Address it immediately before penalties build.*

- **Wage Garnishment:** Money comes straight out of your paycheck.
- **Tax Refund Intercepts:** Federal and state tax refunds can be taken.
- **Credit Reporting:** Late payments hurt your credit score.
- **Seizure of Property or Bank Accounts:** States can freeze or seize funds.

☞ **Survival Tip:** *Always keep records of what you pay. If you pay cash directly to the mother without court records, it often doesn't count.*

~ Chapter 6 ~
Arrears – What Happens When You Fall Behind

Arrears are unpaid child support, also known as "back pay." This is one of the most dangerous traps for fathers, because arrears don't go away once they build up. They continue to grow with interest, penalties, and enforcement actions until paid in full.

"Arrears" means unpaid child support. Once arrears build up, they do not disappear.

- **Interest and Penalties:** Some states add 5–12% interest yearly.
- **Debt to the State:** If the mother received public assistance, you may owe money directly to the government, not her.
- **No Bankruptcy Relief:** Child support arrears cannot be erased through bankruptcy.

How Arrears Build Up
- **Missed Payments:** Every time you miss a payment, the amount is added to your arrears.
- **Interest & Penalties:** Many states add interest (5–12% yearly). Over time, a $5,000 debt can double.
- **Public Assistance Cases:** If the mother received welfare, you may owe the state directly. This debt is often non-negotiable.

Why Arrears Are So Serious
- **No Statute of Limitations:** The debt does not disappear when your child turns 18. The state can pursue you for decades.

- **No Bankruptcy Relief:** Unlike credit cards or loans, child support debt cannot be wiped away by filing bankruptcy.

- **Continued Enforcement:** Arrears keep enforcement agencies active—meaning garnishments, license suspensions, and court hearings continue until it's resolved.

☞ *Scenario: Malik lost his job and didn't go back to court to request a modification. He thought he would "catch up later." After a year, he owed $6,000 in arrears. The state added 9% annual interest. Within three years, his debt climbed to over $10,000. His driver's license was suspended, which made finding stable work harder. Malik's story shows how fast arrears can spiral out of control.*

What To Do If You're Behind
1. **File for a Modification:** If your income drops, ask the court to lower your payment right away.

2. **Set Up a Payment Plan:** Most states allow small, steady payments toward arrears to stop harsher enforcement.

3. **Don't Pay in Cash:** Always pay through official channels so your payments are recorded.

4. **Check for Forgiveness Programs:** Some states forgive debt owed to the state (but usually not to the mother).

☞ **Survival Tip:** *Never ignore arrears. The longer you wait, the worse it gets. Even paying a small amount each month shows effort and can stop the harshest penalties.*

~ Chapter 7 ~
Jail, License Suspension, and Other Consequences

When child support is unpaid, the consequences go beyond garnished wages. States have powerful enforcement tools that can affect your freedom, mobility, and ability to work. These penalties are designed to pressure fathers into paying—but they often create cycles that make it harder to catch up.

Jail Time
- Courts can jail fathers for **"willful nonpayment"**—meaning the judge believes you have the ability to pay but choose not to.
- Jail time is usually short (days to months) but doesn't erase the debt. In fact, arrears continue to grow while you're locked up.
- Getting out often requires a "purge payment," a lump sum you must pay to regain freedom.

License Suspension
- **Driver's License:** Many states suspend your license if you're 3–6 months behind. Without it, commuting to work becomes difficult.
- **Professional Licenses:** If you're a Barber, Contractor, Nurse, or any licensed professional, your ability to work may be suspended.

- **Recreational Licenses:** Hunting and Fishing licenses can also be revoked.

Passport Denial
- If you owe more than $2,500 in arrears, the federal government will deny or revoke your passport. This prevents travel outside the United States.

Credit Reporting
- Arrears are reported to credit agencies, dropping your credit score. This can block you from renting an apartment, buying a car, or qualifying for loans.

☞ **Scenario:** *Anthony fell behind on $4,000 of child support. The state suspended his driver's license and professional electrician license. Without work, his arrears grew faster. When he finally found cash work, the court still threatened jail time unless he paid $1,000 immediately.*

How to Avoid These Consequences
1. **Don't wait.** As soon as you fall behind, request a child support order modification.
2. **Negotiate.** Many states will work with fathers on arrears payment plans.
3. **Show effort.** Even small payments prove you're trying. Judges often spare jail when you show good faith.
4. **Seek help.** Fatherhood programs and legal aid can advocate on your behalf.

☞ **Survival Tip:** *Jail and license suspensions don't solve child support problems—they make them worse. Staying proactive is the only way to avoid these crushing consequences.*

~ Chapter 8 ~
African American Men and the Courtroom – Breaking the Fear

For many African American men, walking into a courtroom feels like stepping into enemy territory. This fear is not imagined—it's rooted in generations of unequal treatment by the justice system. Yet avoiding court is one of the worst mistakes fathers can make in child support cases. Understanding this fear, and learning how to overcome it, is key to surviving the system.

Why Many Avoid Court
- **Historical Distrust:** From slavery to Jim Crow to mass incarceration, the justice system has a long history of disproportionately punishing African American men. This history creates a deep mistrust that continues today.

- **Perceived Bias:** Many African American fathers believe the court automatically sides with mothers, leaving them feeling powerless.

- **Shame and Pride:** Admitting financial struggles in front of a judge can feel humiliating. Some African American men avoid court rather than face that embarrassment.

- **Lack of Resources:** Lawyers are expensive. Without representation, African American fathers fear they'll be railroaded.

The Cost of Avoiding Court

Not showing up doesn't protect you—it hurts you. Judges often issue **default judgments** if a father is absent. These judgments may:

- Assume you earn more than you actually do; leading to unrealistic payment amounts
- Establish paternity without DNA testing
- Create arrears immediately if payments are set too high
-

☞ **Scenario:** *Andre skipped his hearing, thinking the child wasn't his. The judge declared him the father by default and ordered $600 per month in child support based on "estimated income." Andre only made $2,000 a month. Within a year, he was thousands in arrears.*

How to Overcome the Fear

1. **Educate Yourself:** Knowledge of the system reduces intimidation.

2. **Prepare Documents:** Bring pay stubs, bills, and proof of your situation—judges respect facts.

3. **Seek Legal Aid:** Many cities have free or low-cost legal services for fathers.

4. **Stay Calm and Respectful:** Judges notice attitude. Speaking clearly and respectfully goes further than anger or silence.

☞ **Survival Tip:** *The court cannot hear your side if you aren't there. Showing up - even nervous, even unrepresented - gives you a fighting chance.*

☞ **Truth:** *Not showing up makes things worse. Default judgments, higher payments, and lost rights often happen when you don't attend.*

☞ **Survival Tip:** *Show up, stay calm, bring documents, and speak clearly. Courts respect preparation.*

~ Chapter 9 ~
The Debate Over Paternity Tests at Birth

One of the most controversial topics in family law is whether DNA testing should be mandatory at birth. Currently, paternity is often established by a father signing paperwork at the hospital or later in court. But mistakes—or dishonesty—can lock a man into 18 years of child support for a child who may not be biologically his.

The Case for Mandatory Testing

- **Accuracy and Fairness:** DNA tests are over 99% accurate. Automatic testing ensures the right man is identified as the father.

- **Prevents False Paternity:** Studies suggest that in 3–10% of cases, the man listed on the birth certificate is not the biological father. Mandatory testing would prevent these cases.

- **Protects Fathers' Rights:** Men wouldn't have to question later, after years of paying, whether the child is biologically theirs.

The Case Against Mandatory Testing

- **Trust Issues:** Critics argue it sends the message that mothers can't be trusted, potentially straining relationships.

- **Cost and Bureaucracy:** Testing every newborn would require funding and logistics that some argue are unnecessary.

- **Emotional Fallout:** Mandatory testing could create tension in hospitals during an already sensitive time.

☞ **Scenario:** *Clarence signed the hospital paternity acknowledgment without hesitation. Five years later, a DNA test revealed he was not the father. But because he had already been legally recognized, the court refused to undo his obligation. Clarence remains legally responsible for thousands of dollars in arrears.*

What Fathers Should Do Now
- **If you have doubts, request DNA testing immediately.** Don't sign paperwork at the hospital unless you're certain.

- **File a paternity action early.** The longer you wait, the harder it is to challenge.

- **Know your state laws.** Some states allow challenges within a short window—others lock you in permanently.

☞ **Survival Tip:** *Mandatory testing isn't the law (yet). Until it is, the burden falls on fathers to protect themselves. Always confirm before you commit.*

Some argue that all children should be DNA tested at birth. Supporters say this prevents men from being trapped paying for children who aren't theirs. Opponents argue it creates mistrust in relationships.

What it means for you: If you have doubts, request a test early. Once you accept paternity, challenging it later is almost impossible.

~ Chapter 10 ~
Practical Tips for Surviving the System

The child support system is tough, but with preparation and discipline, you can survive it and still be the father your child needs. The key is to be proactive, organized, and consistent. Here are practical strategies every father should know.

Stay Organized
- Keep **all paperwork**: court orders, receipts, payment records, and communications with the other parent.
- Create a dedicated folder or binder so you can bring documents to court at a moment's notice.
- Use official payment channels (state agencies or money orders) to ensure proof of payment.

Communicate the Right Way
- Keep communication with the other parent **respectful and documented** (text or email is best).
- Avoid verbal agreements that can't be proven in court.
- If problems arise (like visitation issues), address them through court - not by withholding support.

Financial Survival Tips
- **Budget realistically.** Treat child support like rent—it must be paid first.

- **Plan ahead.** Set aside money weekly so payments don't feel overwhelming at the end of the month.
- **Avoid arrears.** Even a small, consistent payment is better than nothing.

☞ **Scenario:** *Devon struggled after his hours were cut at work. Instead of ignoring payments, he filed for a modification. The court reduced his monthly payment, and he set up a $25/month arrears plan. Because Devon stayed proactive, he avoided license suspension and jail.*

Checklist: If You're Served Court Papers
1. **Read carefully.** Know your court date and what's being asked.
2. **Respond on time.** Missing deadlines = default judgment.
3. **Gather documents.** Paystubs, bills, and proof of expenses.
4. **Request DNA testing** if paternity is in question.
5. **Show up prepared.** Dress neatly, speak respectfully, and stick to facts.

☞ **Survival Tip:** *Judges respect fathers who show responsibility—even when struggling. Effort counts. Showing up, paying what you can, and staying consistent keeps the system from crushing you.*

- Always show up for court dates.
- Ask for child support order modifications if you lose your job or your income changes.

- Stay respectful in court, even if you feel the system is unfair.
- Pay through official channels (not cash in hand).
- Build a relationship with your child outside of money—time and presence matter.

Michael T. Logan

~ Chapter 11 ~
Conclusion – Taking Control of Your Future

Child support may feel like a punishment, but it's really about responsibility. By understanding the system, African American men can protect their rights, avoid traps, and remain present in their childrens' lives.

Surviving the child support system isn't easy—but it is possible. This guide has shown that child support is not just about money. It's about knowledge, preparation, and responsibility. Too many African American men are crushed by a system they don't fully understand, but you don't have to be one of them.

You've learned how child support came to be, how paternity is established, the difference between custody and support, the dangers of arrears, and the severe consequences of ignoring court. You've seen why so many men fear the courtroom, and how that fear often backfires. You've also explored the debate over mandatory paternity testing, and most importantly, you've gained survival strategies to stay ahead of the system.

The lesson is simple: **knowledge is survival.** When you understand how the system works, you can protect yourself from its harshest penalties. By staying proactive—showing up for court, keeping records, paying what you can, and seeking modifications when necessary—you can avoid traps that destroy lives.

☞ **Scenario:** *Jamal was terrified when he got his first court summons. Instead of hiding, he prepared—he brought proof of* *his income, requested a DNA test, and filed for visitation rights at the same time. His support order was fair, his visitation was granted, and he avoided arrears by staying consistent. Jamal's story is proof that knowledge and preparation change everything.*

Moving Forward

This book isn't just about surviving child support—it's about reclaiming control of your life. Children need more than money. They need fathers who are present, consistent, and empowered. Even within a system that feels unfair, you can take steps that protect your future and strengthen your bond with your child(ren).

☞ **Survival Tip:** *Never give up. Even if you've fallen behind or made mistakes, it's never too late to step up, learn the system, and fight for your role as a father.*

✏️ Author's Note:

From one man who has seen the struggles up close - I wrote this guide so you don't have to walk into court blind. My hope is that you not only survive child support, but also emerge stronger, wiser, and more determined to be the father your child(ren) deserves. Remember: The system is hard, but knowledge is survival.

– Michael T. Logan

www.ingramcontent.com/pod-product-compliance
Lightning Source LLC
Chambersburg PA
CBHW030124170426
43198CB00009B/729